SUSANA PENTLAND

Cyber Security for All : Kids

*Be Brave, Be Smart, Be a Safe Cyber Hero. A Fun Guide
to Cyber Security For Kids.*

ZANI PUBLISHING

First published by ZANI PUBLISHING 2025

First edition

ISBN: 9798307184882

This book was professionally typeset on Reedsy.
Find out more at reedsy.com

This book is dedicated to Hudson-Ray,
with love from your mum of awesome cyberness 🖤

Every hero has a super power!

Yours is knowing how to stay safe online.

🌟 Stay smart.
🌟 Stay kind.
🌟 Stay curious.
🌟 Stay awesome in all things cyberness.

- Susana 🖤

Contents

Introduction

Welcome to the Cyber World!

Have you ever played word games, seen cartoon shows like Bluey or Number Blocks or Paw-Patrol? Have you ever done a Face time with family and friends using a computer or mobile phone on the internet?

This is Cyber.

Cyber is all things to do with computers (including tablets and phones) and the internet. The internet can sometimes be called "The Web" or being "online". It is like a giant, playground where you can learn, play, and explore so many fun things!

But just like in a real playground, there are some important rules to follow to keep yourself safe and happy. Together, we'll learn how to become Cyber Safety Heroes who are super brave, super smart, and ready to take on the online world with super confidence.

So get your hero cape and let's get started on this fun adventure!

What to Expect in This Guide:
   ☆ Learn how to create your own secret superhero identity.
   ☆ Discover the magic of strong passwords, which are the keys to your treasure chest!
   ☆ Spot sneaky tricky cyber villains and learn how to outsmart them.
   ☆ Explore the online digital world, safely, kinder, and super smarter.
   Ready to join the Cyber Heroes team?

Let's go!

How To Use This Guide

Welcome to the *Cyber Security For All KIDS Guide!*

Congratulations for taking this step towards protecting your little person and gearing them up for confidence, and the smarts to navigate the cyber world safely.

This guide is your family's essential toolkit for teaching kids under 10 how to explore the online world safely and confidently.

Here's how to make the most of this guide:

✨ *Take It One Chapter at a Time*

The internet is a big, exciting place, and learning to navigate it safely can feel overwhelming for kids. That's why this guide is designed to be read one chapter at a time. Each chapter introduces a new topic, like creating strong passwords or spotting online risks, in a simple and fun way that's easy to understand.

By focusing on one chapter at a time:

- Kids can absorb the lessons without feeling rushed or overloaded.
- Parents and kids can discuss each topic together, answering questions and sharing thoughts.
- You can build a solid foundation for online safety step by step.

✨ *Reinforce Learning with Fun Activities*

At the end of each chapter, you'll find a practical, hands-on activity that turns the lesson into an exciting adventure! These activities are designed to:

- **Make Learning Fun:** Whether it's creating a superhero badge or drawing a safe online map, kids will enjoy engaging with the material in a creative way.
- **Encourage Collaboration:** These activities are perfect for kids and parents to do together, fostering teamwork and trust.
- **Build Confidence:** By practicing what they've learned, kids will feel empowered to use their new skills in the real world.

✰ Tips for Parents

Take your time! Allow kids to fully grasp each chapter before moving on to the next.

Use the activities as opportunities to connect with your child, ask questions, share examples, and have fun.

Celebrate small wins, like when your child remembers an online safety rule or creates a strong password.

Chapter 1: The Internet

Hello, little explorer! Imagine the internet is just like a big magical universe that connects computers, phones, and tablets all over the world.

The Internet Is Also Like a Library, A Fun Park, And A Letter Box all in one!

The internet helps us:

☆ **Learn new things**: Find out about dinosaurs, spaceships and space travel, or how rainbows are made.

☆ **Have fun**: Watch shows, play games, and listen to your favorite songs.

☆ **Stay in touch**: Send messages, video chat, or share pictures with family and friends.

But just like when you go outside, there are rules to keep you safe when you explore online.

THINK BEFORE YOU CLICK

THINK BEFORE YOU CLICK

There are some rules to keep you safe when you explore online.

How to Stay Safe on the Internet

☆ **Use safe websites**: Ask your parents to help you choose websites that are fun and safe, like ABC Kids or National Geographic Kids.

☆ **Ask before you click**: If something pops up and you're not sure what it is, ask a grown-up before clicking.

☆ **Stay in kid-friendly places**: Use apps and games made just for kids.

For Example:

Imagine the internet is like a big amusement park. Some rides are super fun and perfect for kids, but some rides might be too scary or dangerous.

Your grown-ups can guide you to the best and safest ride, just like they help you find safe websites!

FUN ACTIVITY

Make Your Own Internet Adventure Map!

✐ Get some paper and crayons or markers.

✐ Draw a magical land that shows your favorite websites as fun places, like a "YouTube Kids Castle" or "Learning Island."

✐ Add warning signs for unsafe places, like "Danger! Pop-ups here!"

✐ Show your map to your family and explain how it helps you stay safe online.

Chapter 2: Protect Your Super Secret Identity!

Welcome back super hero!

Did you know you have your very own secret identity?

Your Identity Is Unique And Special To You.

Identity information is all the special things about you, that make you

☆YOU☆

Things like your name, your birthday, your school or kindy, your medical records, and even where you live. Keeping all these details safe is super important. So let's learn how to protect your secret identity together!

What Is Your Secret Identity?

Your secret identity is:
- ➡ Your name.
- ➡ Your age and birthday.
- ➡ Where you live or go to school.
- ➡ Your phone number or passwords.

These are special and belong only to you and your family. Sharing them online with anyone you don't really know that well can cause big deep trouble.

We would not want that!

☆ *Protect Your Secret Identity*

Why Is It Important to Protect Your Identity?

Imagine if everyone knew that Spider Man was really Peter Parker. The bad guys would easily find him and cause big trouble! They could make trouble at his home, or wait for him at his work place to do bad things. They could make a robbery while he was away and steal important things.

The same thing happens online.

If you share too much information, strangers might:
- ✗ Try to trick you.
- ✗ Pretend to be your friend to learn more.
- ✗ Use your information to cause problems.

That's why it's important to keep your personal details a secret.

How to Keep Your Identity Safe

☆ Use a superhero nickname: Instead of using your real name, pick a fun nickname like "GamerStar123" or "KittyHero."

☆ Keep personal info private. Don't share your address, phone number, or school name with anyone online, even if they seem nice.

☆ Ask your adults before sharing photos online. Always check with your parents' permission.

☆ Tell a grown-up: If anyone asks for your information or makes you feel unsure, tell a parent or teacher right away.

For Example

Imagine you are playing hide-and-seek.

You would not yell out, "Oi!! I'm hiding in the garden!" because then you would get found easily, and then out of the game.

The same goes for your identity online. Keeping your identity details secret keeps you safe and in the game!

FUN ACTIVITY

Objective: Help kids understand the importance of data privacy and privacy settings.

Design Your Very Own Super Hero Badge!

Make Your Superhero Identity Badge!

➡ Grab some paper and markers or crayons.

➡ Draw a badge with your superhero name, like "Cornetto Steve", "Lightning Llama", "Cyber Ninja".

➡ Make it with bright fun shapes like ☆, ϟ or ♥

➡ Show your cool badge to everyone, and how it's safe.

Privacy Settings Puzzle

Make a puzzle with pieces that explain ways to stay safe, like:

➡ Keep your profile private.

➡ Turn off location sharing.

➡ When you put the puzzle together, it forms a picture of a locked safe!

Chapter 3: Passwords - Your Secret Code

Did you know passwords are like secret codes?

They help protect your favorite pictures, messages and important details about your identity.

Let's learn why they're so important and how to make strong ones no one can guess!

Always Protect Your Passwords, these are your precious gems and secret codes!

Why Are Passwords So Important?

Passwords keep your things safe online, just like a key with padlock protects a treasure chest.

If someone guesses your password, they could:
🔐 Mess with your games.
🔐 Look at your private pictures or messages.
🔐 Pretend to be you and cause trouble.

🔐 *It will be up to you to choose your own passwords.*

A strong password should:
✔ be at least **12 characters long.**
✔ have a mix of **BIG letters, small letters, numbers, and symbols like @, # or %**
✗ never be a word easily found in a dictionary.
✗ never be the name of a family member, or your pet, a product, or brands

⭐ Keep your passwords safe, like you would with a treasure chest. Only you (and your trusted grown-up) should know your secret code!

Tips for Making Strong Passwords Harder to Guess

⭐ **Make it long**: At least 12 letters, numbers, or symbols. Longer is best!

⭐ **Mix it up**: Use big letters and small letters, numbers, and symbols like @ or #.

⭐ **Add a fun twist**: Think of something you remember, like "I love cats," and turn it into a fun code like "1Lov3C@ts." This is also called a Passphrase.

⭐ **No easy stuff**: Do not use your name, your pet's name, "1234," or "password." That's too simple!

How to Keep Your Passwords Safe

⭐ **Never share it!** Only tell your trusted parents if they need to know.

⭐ **Don't write it any where others will see.** Hide it in a safe spot, or let your parents hide it for you.

⭐ **Change it if someone finds it.** Ask a grown-up to help you "reset" your password or make a new password.

An Example

Imagine you have a diary with all your secrets. Would you leave the key where anyone could find it?

No way! Keep it hidden and safe!

🔐 *Your Password Is Like The Key To Your Diary.*

FUN ACTIVITY

Objective: Teach kids how to create strong passwords.

Password Treasure Hunt!

🎨 Draw a treasure chest on a piece of paper.

🎨 Inside the chest, write a pretend password using the rules:

➡ At least 8 characters.

➡ A mix of letters, numbers, and symbols.

➡ Something fun or secret, like your favorite animal or food.

➡ Example: "TacoLover@22" or "PandaP@ws99."

🎨 Add decorations like jewels, coins, or anything that makes your treasure chest sparkle!

🎨 Show everyone your drawing and explain why your password is strong and secret.

Create a Strong Password Challenge

✏ Write different passwords on cards, such as "1234," "mypassword," and "SunSh1ne!2#".

✏ Guess which passwords are strong and why (long, includes letters, numbers, and symbols).

✏ Challenge kids to come up with their own strong passwords.

✏ For added fun, turn it into a game: roll a dice to decide the number of characters, or pick a favorite animal, add numbers or symbols!

Chapter 4: Online Safety

⭐ *Online Safety Means Making Smart Choices.*

Being safe online means taking care before clicking or thinking smarter. By making smarter choices, you can continue to have your fun and stay safe while using the internet.

Why Is Online Safety So Important?

Being safe online protects you from:
- ✅ Strangers who might not be nice.
- ✅ Scary or bad things you don't want to see.
- ✅ People trying to take your information.

Your Digital Footprint

A **digital footprint** is like little footprints you leave behind when you walk on sand, but instead of sand, it's on the internet.

Every time you play a game, watch a video, listen to music, visit a website or use a computer, you leave tiny marks that show where you've been and what you've done.

These marks allow others to see where you have been or what you like, so it's important to be careful and only leave good, safe footprints.

Some of these marks in your digital footprint can be cleaned up, like erasing chalk on a board. For example, you can delete posts, photos, or videos you've shared - IF no one else has saved them already. But if they have, these marks can not be undone. It's there to stay in the online world forever, like paints that doesn't wash off. That's because other people or websites, might save what you shared.. and there is no stopping this.

So, it's always best to think carefully before leaving any evidence of marks online!

Tips for Staying Safe Online

☆ Don't talk to strangers: Just like in real life, only talk to people you know.

☆ Tell a grown-up: If something makes you feel worried or confused, talk to a parent, teacher, or another trusted adult.

☆ Ask before you share: Always check with your parents before posting pictures or information.

☆ Stay in safe spaces: Use websites and apps made for kids.

☆ **Be kind with nice words and treat others with respect always.**

An Example

Imagine the internet is a big park. You would not walk off alone or talk to strangers, right?

The same goes for being online, stick with safe spaces and people you know in real life.

FUN ACTIVITY

Objective: Teach kids about their online presence and being safe.

Design a Safety Shield!

✏ Draw a big shield on paper and divide it into sections. In each section, write or draw one safety tip (like "Don't talk to strangers" or "Ask a grown-up for help").

✏ Decorate your shield with bright colors and stickers to make it uniquely yours. Show your shield to your family and explain how each tip keeps you safe online.

Draw Your Digital Footprint

✐ Explore what is meant by digital footprint online.

✐ Draw a footprint on paper and fill it with all things that apply with your digital footprint online. It might be websites visited, pictures shared, music listened to or videos watched, even chatting to family overseas.

✐ Discuss how to keep their footprint safe and positive.

What Does Your Digital Footprint Look Like?

Chapter 5: Watch Out for Cyber Villains!

Always Look Out For Cyber Villains

Did you know there are villains on the internet too? But don't worry! You now have super hero power plays to stop them.

Cyber villains are the sneaky naughty little mites (the baddies) who will try to trick you or mess with your online fun.

Cyber Villains Are Annoying Sneaky Naughty Baddies On The Internet.

What Is a Cyber Villain?

They can be:

➡ Phishing: Fake messages, websites or emails pretending to be real, like "You've won a prize! Click here!" or "You need to change your password, click this link"

➡ Scams: Ads or links promising free stuff but really stealing your info
details.

➡ Cyberbullies: People who send mean messages online.

➡ Fake Friends: Strangers pretending to be your friend, or someone else to get your secrets.

How to Spot A Cyber Villain

Be a detective and look for:

🔎 Messages asking for your password or personal info.

🔎 Links that look weird with lots of numbers and symbols.

🔎 Promises like "Get free game coins now!"

🔎 Strangers asking you too many questions.

Tips to Outsmart Cyber Villains

⭐ **Keep your secret!** Don't share your name, address, or passwords.

⭐ **Think before you click,** if something seems fishy, don't click!

⭐ **Block and tell.** Block mean people and tell an adult.

⭐ **Stay in safe spaces,** only use websites your parents say are okay.

⭐ **Ask for help** if you're unsure, adults are here to help.

WATCH OUT FOR CYBER VILLAINS.

An Example

Imagine someone at a carnival says, "I'll give you free candy if you tell me your secrets." Would you trust them? Of course not! Online, if someone asks for personal info or promises something amazing, it's probably a trick.

FUN ACTIVITY

Objective: Help kids recognize phishing messages and scams.

Spot the Cyber Villain!

✍ Draw a picture of a superhero (that's you!) protecting the internet from villains.

✍ Add different cyber villains to your drawing, like:

➡ A trickster holding a fake email.

➡ A bully sending mean messages.

➡ A scammer offering fake prizes.

✍ Show how you use your superhero powers to stop them, like blocking or using a safety shield!

Phishing Detective Game

🔍 Look at pretend messages with clues that they're scams.

🔍 Highlight red flags like "Click here to win!" or asking for personal info.

🔍 Turn it into a game—circle the clues and explain why they're tricky!

Chapter 6: Safe Online Gaming

Playing games in real life can be loads of fun.

You can explore new things, learn new things, solve puzzles, and have the best time playing with friends.

There are some basic rules to follow, to stay safe while you play.

Let's learn how to play smart!

What Is Online Gaming?

Online gaming is like playing pretend games, but you do it on a computer, or a tablet, or on a phone. You can explore magical worlds, solve puzzles, or race cars.

You can play a game on your own, or sometimes you can play with other people online. It's important to be kind, take turns, and stay safe!

You can play by yourself, or with many friends, or even with other people from around the world.

Some games let you also chat with other, even players we don't know in real life from a different part of the world. So to stay safe, it's very important to be careful and smart, who we are really talking to and what details we are sharing.

What Are the Risks?

Cyber risks are like little dangers or tricky problems that can happen when using the internet, like sneaky bugs in a game or strangers pretending to be nice.

They can hide in things like fake messages, tricky links, or unsafe websites. That's why it's important to always ask a grown-up for help and stick to safe places online!

Here are some things to watch out for:

✕ Strangers: Some players might not be who they say they are.

✕ Mean Messages: Sometimes, people can say unkind things.

✕ Weird Messages: Sometimes bad people hang out in gaming chat rooms, to trick you into doing or sending stuff about yourself. They make out they are friends your age, but really they are big bad adults behaving wrongly. They may even send you weird photos or talk about private things that make you feel uncomfortable.

✕ Scams: Links like "Free skins!" or "Win coins now!" may be tricks.

✕ Too Much Time: Playing too long can make you tired.

Tips to Stay Safe While Gaming

- ✓ Don't chat with strangers. Only talk to people you know in real life.
- ✓ Keep secrets safe. Don't share your name, school, or passwords.
- ✓ Block mean players. If someone is unkind, being rude or saying weird or nasty things, block them and tell an adult.
- ✓ Be kind. Treat others how you want to be treated.
- ✓ Take breaks. After 20–30 minutes, stretch and rest your eyes.
- ✓ Ask before downloading. Always check with a parent first.
- ✓ Tell a grown-up. If something feels wrong, ask for help.

For Example

Imagine you're at the park.

Would you talk to strangers or play all day without resting?

No way!

You could really hurt yourself playing all day with no rest or get into big trouble talking with strangers.

It's the same with online gaming. Stick to friends you know in real life.

FUN ACTIVITY

Objective: Teach kids to distinguish between safe and unsafe online behaviors.

Design Your Gaming Superhero!

✎ Draw yourself as a gaming superhero!

✎ Add gadgets like:

➡ A "Privacy Shield" to hide your info.

➡ A "Time Tracker" to remind you to take breaks.

➡ A "Kindness Ray" to spread good vibes!

✎ Name your superhero and share your favorite safety tip with your family.

Safe or Not? Sorting Game

Make two buckets labeled "Safe" and "Not Safe."

Write actions on cards, like:

➡ "Sharing your password."

➡ "Asking a parent before downloading."

Sort the cards and explain why each action is safe or not.

☆ *Parents Play Key Roles To Ensure Their Kids Are Safe Online.*

Here are some extra tips to help:

Research Games Together:

☆ Look for games with age-appropriate content, clear ratings, and reviews from trusted sources like *Common Sense Media*.

☆ Play the game with your child to understand its features and potential risks.

Enable Parental Controls:

☆ Set up parental controls on gaming platforms to manage playtime, restrict purchases, and block inappropriate content.

☆ Use features like chat filters or disable in-game chat to limit communication with strangers.

Encourage Open Conversations:

☆ Talk to your child about their gaming experiences, what they love about the game and who they're playing with.

☆ Make it clear they can come to you if they feel uncomfortable or encounter a problem online.

Set Clear Rules:

☆ Create a family gaming plan with limits on screen time, approved games, and designated play times.

☆ Keep gaming devices in shared spaces like the living room to monitor game play easily.

Teach Digital Citizenship:

⭐ Reinforce kindness and respect when interacting with others online.

⭐ Explain the importance of not sharing any personal identifiable information (PII) with anyone they encounter in online games.

Chapter 7: Cyber Bullying - Be Kind Online

Be Kind Always 🖤

What is Cyber Bullying?

Cyber bullying is when someone is mean or hurtful to others using the internet, like sending mean messages or saying unkind words in a game.

It happens when ever you are online and can be:

➡ Sending mean messages.

➡ Sharing pictures to embarrass someone.

➡ Saying unkind things online.

Cyber bullying can happen in online games, on social media, or in chats.

× It's not nice.

× It can make you feel sad or scared.

× It feels awful.

How to Spot Cyber Bullying

Look out for these signs:

🔎 Mean or rude messages sent to you or others.

🔎 Someone posting hurtful pictures or videos.

🔎 Comments online that make you feel upset or worried.

Be A Kindness Warrior ☆

What to Do If Cyber Bullying Happens

You are never alone!

If cyber bullying happens:
- ✓ Tell a trusted Grown-Up, a parent, or teacher as they can help.
- ✓ Don't reply, often bullies want to see you upset. They just want a reaction from you. Ignore all their messages.
- ✓ Block these bullies online so they can't bother you again.
- ✓ Save the proof if it's really bad. Take screenshots or save messages to show an adult.

How to Prevent or Stop Cyber bullying

✔ Be kind online always, by treating others how you want to be treated. If you wouldn't say something in person, don't say it online.

✔ Help others if they are being bullied, speak up or tell an adult. It's important to be a good friend and stand up for others in need.

✔ Don't post anything that could be offensive or hurt others feelings. Always ask yourself: "Would I want someone to say this to me?"

☆ *We Can All Take Part In Stopping Cyber Bullying.*

Tips to Be Kind Online and Offline

✓ Share nice comments to others, it always brings a smile.
It's also a great way to make new friends and be more likable.

✓ Apologize if you accidentally hurt someone's feelings. We all make
mistakes so it's important to say sorry and help fix things.

✓ Help others when you see them upset. Saying "Are you okay?" can
really make others feel much better.

☆ *Remember Golden Rule: 'Treat Others How You Would Want To Be Treated'.*

An Example:

Imagine you are playing online words game, and a player says "Haha-You loser!" or " You are stupid" or "You Suck!". This is cyber bullying. Instead of saying something mean back, simply mute or block them. Tell a grown-up, and they'll know how to help.

FUN ACTIVITY

⭐ *Combat Cyber Bullying With Empathy And Kindness.*

Draw Your Kindness Circle!

Here's a fun activity to remind us all how important kindness is.

✏ Grab a piece of paper and draw a big circle in the middle.

✏ Write down all the ways you can be kind online and offline around the circle (like saying nice things, helping others, or sharing smiles).

✏ Inside the circle, draw yourself smiling or doing something kind!

You can even color it in and hang it up as a reminder to be kind every day, both online and offline!

💜 *Being Kind To Others Makes The Internet And The World A Better Place!*

Cyber bullying Role Play

💜 Role-play scenarios where one child pretends to receive a mean comment online, and the other offers kind words or asks a grown-up for help.

💜 Discuss how to handle bullying, how to be kind online, and the importance of reporting bad behavior.

Chapter 8: Getting Help from Your Grown-Up Sidekicks

✫ *Every Super Hero Has A Sidekick*

Why You Need Your Trusty Grown Up Sidekicks

When you're exploring the online world, it's always a good idea to have your grown-up to guide you. They're always ready to protect you and make sure your online adventures are fun and safe!

These are your trusted parents or family members, teachers, or other family members. They are there to keep you safe.

Just like asking for help with tricky homework, you can ask for help online too, and that's totally cool!

When Should You Ask for Help?

If something online makes you feel unsafe, uncomfortable, scared, or unsure, tell a grown-up right away.

How Grown Ups Help You Stay Safe

☑ Privacy Settings: Grown-ups can make sure only friends can see your online stuff—like a special lock on your account.

☑ Safe Sharing: They teach you what is safe to share or not.

☑ Help If someone is nasty or something is strange.

An Example

Imagine you find a fun game online. Before you play, you ask a grown-up to check if it's safe. They can check that it's safe from strangers.

FUN ACTIVITY

Design Your Super Sidekick Badge

🖊 Draw a badge with your sidekick's name (like "Mum" or "Teacher").

🖊 Write how they help keep you safe online.

🖊 Decorate it with all the colors and stickers!

Family Cyber Safety Plan

🖊 Work with your family to create online rules, like how much time to spend online or what sites are safe to visit.

🖊 Decorate the plan with stickers and drawings for each rule!

Chapter 9: Screen Time Balance For Fun & Play

What is Screen Time?

Screen time is the time you spend on devices like the TV, or tablets, a phone, or computers to learn, watch or play things. Playing online games, watching videos, and talking to friends online all count as screen time.

It's like having a 'fun turn' with these devices, but it's important to take breaks to drink water, play, read, have a meal and run around too!

It can be fun or educational, but too much screen time will hurt your eyes, your head and your health.

It will also take away time from other super fun things like riding your bike, playing outside, visiting friends, going swimming, cooking with mum or drawing with Granny.

Why Is Screen Time Management Important?

Think of your day like a yummy plate of food.

You need a healthy balance - a mix of everything to feel great!

If you spend too much time on screens -

✗ Your eyes will hurt. Over time, this will damage your eyes and give you blurry vision.

✗ You miss out on all the fun with friends, playing, running, using your imagination (which are the key building blocks to problem solving and critical thinking)

✗ You will mess up your sleeping.

✗ Make you a little kranky-pants! You will feel grumpy and really short upset over time. And this is no fun for anyone. Especially for your Mummy!

By balancing screen time, all the time, and you will be healthier and feel happier!

How to Balance Screen Time with Other Activities

☑ **Take Breaks**: After 30 minutes, stretch like a superhero or grab a healthy snack.

☑ **Go Outside**: Run, ride your bike, or play your favorite outdoor game. Fresh air is amazing!

☑ **Be Creative**: Draw, paint, build with blocks, or read a book. Let your imagination shine!

☑ **Family Time**: Play board games, bake cakes or talk about your day.

Tips for Safe and Healthy Screen Time

⏰ **Set a Timer**: Make it a game to stop when the timer beeps.

⏰ **Stay in Safe Spaces**: Only use apps or games your grown-ups say are okay.

⏰ **No Screens 1 Hour Before Bed**: Wind down with quiet time or story time for sweet dreams and restful sleep.

⏰ **Choose Fun, Educational, Empowering, Smart Content**: Go for learning shows or games that make you smarter so you grow to be the best version of you!

An Example

Let's pretend you've been playing an online game or watching videos for a while. Your legs feel tired, and your head feels a bit fuzzy. What should you do?

- ⏰ Pause the game and stretch like you're reaching for the stars.
- ⏰ Grab a ball or favorite toy and head outside to play.
- ⏰ When you come back, you'll feel fresh and ready for more fun!

SAFE ONLINE SCREEN TIME
BALANCE FUN AND PLAY

FUN ACTIVITY

Design Your Dream Day Planner!

Let's make a fun day planner to balance screen time and other activities.

✍ Take a piece of paper and draw a big rectangle for the day.

✍ Put 3 parts for "Morning," "Afternoon," and "Evening."

✍ In each part, draw or write activities you like to do. For example:

➡ Morning: Draw a sun for outdoor play.

➡ Afternoon: Draw a tablet or computer for screen time.

➡ Evening: Draw a book or star for bedtime reading

✍ Colour your planner, make it exciting then put it where you see it every day!

CYBER
SAFETY

Conclusion: Now You Are A Cyber Safety Hero!

You've learned how to:

⭐ Stay safe and kind online.

⭐ Protect your personal information.

⭐ Keep your screen time balanced.

⭐ *Grab your Cyber Hero cape and explore the internet safely! Remember, if you're ever unsure about any thing online, ask your grown-up for help.*

FUN ACTIVITY

Objective: Encourage creativity while reinforcing cyber security lessons. Reinforce online safety rules.

Design a Cyber Safety Poster

- Grab paper, crayons, markers, or even a computer drawing program.
- Ask kids to create a poster with a slogan like, "Be Kind Online!" or "Think Before You Click!"
- Include pictures of kids being safe online, like using strong passwords or asking an adult for help.
- Display the posters in a classroom or at home as a daily reminder.

Online Safety Scavenger Hunt

🔍 Create a scavenger hunt with clues that teach online safety. For example:

➡ "Find something that helps you stay safe online" (Answer: privacy settings).

➡ "Find an example of a strong password."

➡ "Spot the difference between a trusted app and a fake one."

🔍 Win a small prize for completing the hunt.

Cyber Super Hero Story Time

✔ Have kids create their own cyber superhero who protects people online.

✔ They can draw their superhero and write a short story about how they save the day from cyberbullies, phishing emails, or unsafe websites.

✔ Share the stories with others to inspire teamwork and creativity.

☆ *Make Up Your Very Own Cyber Super Hero Story*

Parents Corner

Handy Tips for Parents

Here is a starting point of practical tips and basic insights to help support your child's journey towards online safety, cyber literacy and digital etiquette.

✓ Understanding the Digital World with continual awareness

- **What Kids Do Online:** Be present with your kids when they are on screentime, see what activities they enjoy, which are their favourite videos, or who which friends they like chatting to.
- **Potential Risks:** Simple explanations of dangers like cyber bullying, scams, and exposure to inappropriate content.

✓ Establish Safe Digital Practices and Ground Rules: Set the screen time limits, be really clear on this and be consistent. There's a lot of confluence among the studies and research on the negative impacts of excessive screen time and the developing brain in young children (on any devices, the phone, tablet, computer, TV). Such results have shown negative impacts include:

✗ Cognitive and Brain Development

- **Delayed Language and Social Skills:** Increased screen exposure, especially passive consumption, can reduce interactions with caregivers and peers, leading to slower language development.

- **Attention Issues**: High screen exposure, particularly fast-paced and overstimulating content, can contribute to shorter attention spans and difficulties focusing.
- **Lower Academic Performance**: Excessive screen use can displace activities that support cognitive growth, such as reading, problem-solving, and creative play.

× Emotional and Behavioral Issues

- **Increased Anxiety and Depression**: Excessive screen time, especially on social media or highly stimulating apps, has been linked to higher rates of anxiety, depression, and emotional dysregulation.
- **Impulse Control Problems**: Overuse of screens, particularly in gaming, can lead to difficulty in self-regulation and impulse control.
- **Reduced Ability to Manage Frustration**: Fast-paced digital experiences can create expectations for instant gratification, making real-world patience and resilience harder to develop.

× Physical Health Concerns

- **Sleep Disruptions**:The blue light emitted by screens can suppress melatonin production, leading to lack of sleep impacting brain and body development and muscle recovery.
- **Obesity and Poor Posture**: Prolonged sedentary screen use reduces physical activity, increasing the risk of obesity, poor muscle development, and postural issues.
- **Eye Strain and Headaches**: Digital screens contribute to digital eye strain, headaches, and potential long-term vision problems.

✕ Social Development and Family Bonding

- **Reduced Empathy and Social Skills**: Less face-to-face interaction can weaken a child's ability to read social cues, regulate emotions, and develop empathy.
- **Weakened Parent-Child Attachment**: Excessive screen use may reduce meaningful interactions with parents, which are crucial for emotional security.
- **Decreased Outdoor and Free Play**: Screen time can replace activities like imaginative play, problem-solving with peers, and nature exploration, all vital for holistic development.

✕ Addiction and Dopamine Dependency

- **Tech Addiction**: Overexposure to digital entertainment, especially highly stimulating content (e.g., fast-paced cartoons, games, or social media), can create a dependency on dopamine-driven engagement. (Addiction and all the side affects that go along with this!!)
- **Reduced Interest in Offline Activities**: Children who are constantly engaged with screens may find offline activities boring and struggle to engage in less stimulating tasks.

✓ Create an approved list of websites and apps.

✓ Set boundaries for online communication (e.g., only talking to friends they know in real life).

✓ **Use Parental Controls:** Activate safety settings on devices, browsers, and apps. Enable content filters and monitoring tools.

✓ **Reinforce Key Cyber Security Skills**
- **Personal Information:** Emphasize the importance of keeping personal details private (e.g., no sharing names, addresses, or passwords).
- **Strong Passwords:** Encourage kids to create and use strong passwords, and explain why they shouldn't share them.
- **Critical Thinking:** Teach kids to question unexpected messages, links, or offers that seem "too good to be true."

✓ **Encouraging Open Communication**

- **Be Approachable:** Let kids know they can come to you without fear of punishment if something feels wrong online.
- **Ask Questions:** Regularly check in with your child about their online experiences.
- **Listen First:** Respond with calm and be supportive if your child encounters a problem.

✅ Building Digital Citizenship

- **Be Kind Online:** Teach kids the importance of using polite and kind language in chats or comments.
- **Recognizing Cyber bullying:** Discuss what cyber bullying looks like and how to handle it (e.g., save messages, block bullies, report to an adult).
- **Sharing Responsibly:** Remind kids to only post pictures or videos they'd be comfortable showing to anyone.

✅ Tools and Resources for Parents

- **Apps and Software:** Recommend tools for monitoring and protecting kids online, like parental controls, screen time trackers, and web filters.
- **Trusted Websites:** Provide a list of kid-friendly sites and platforms (e.g., PBS Kids, YouTube Kids).
- **Educational Resources:** Suggest online resources to help parents learn more about internet safety (e.g., NetSmartz, Common Sense Media).

✅ Modeling Good Behavior

- **Lead by Example:** Show responsible cyber habits by practicing what you preach (e.g., limit screen time, avoiding oversharing).

- **Family Time Offline:** Emphasize the importance of balance by setting aside time for non-digital activities like reading, outdoor play, or board games.

✅ Creating a Family Cyber Safety Plan

- **Collaborate:** Work together to write down clear rules about using devices, apps, and the internet.
- **Emergency Steps:** Outline what to do if something goes wrong online, like identifying trusted adults to inform or reporting the issue.
- **Review Regularly:** Update your family's plan as kids grow and their online activities evolve.

✅ Understand the Benefits of Technology

- **Highlight Benefits:** Acknowledge the educational and social opportunities the internet provides, such as learning new skills or connecting with family.
- **Encourage Exploration:** Let kids try new online activities in safe, supervised ways.

✔ Staying Informed

- **Keep Up with Emerging Risks, Tech and Trends:** Learn about popular apps, new trending games, and platforms your child uses.
- **Stay Educated:** Attend workshops or read guides on the latest cyber security best practices for families.

Safe Games for Kids Under 10

Here are some safe games that are known to be age-appropriate for Children under 10 yrs old, which are educational, interactive and fun.

➡ **PBS Kids Games**

- Offers a wide variety of educational games based on popular PBS shows like *Sesame Street, Elmo* and *Curious George.*
- Suitable for early learning (math, reading, problem-solving).
- Website: www.pbskids.org

➡ **ABCmouse**

- A subscription-based platform with fun, interactive games that teach reading, math, and science.
- Tailored for preschool to early elementary levels.
- Website: www.plus.abcmouse.com

➡ **Nick Jr. Games**

- Features interactive and colorful games with characters like Dora the Explorer and PAW Patrol.
- Includes learning-focused activities for young kids.
- Website : www.nick.com/games

➡ **RStarfall**

- Focuses on literacy, phonics, and early math skills.
- Engaging for preschoolers and young children.

- Website : www.starfall.com

➡ Toca Boca Games

- Offers creative and exploratory games like *Toca Kitchen* or *Toca Life.*
- Encourages imaginative play in safe, offline environments.
- Website : www.tocaboca.com

➡ ABCya! Educational Games

- Combines learning and fun with a variety of math, reading, and logic-based games.
- Website : www.abcya.com

About the Author

Born in Bali and orphaned until the age of four, Susana's life transformed when she was adopted by an Australian family. Over the past two decades she has built a diverse professional portfolio spanning operations, business, sales and administration, with now an emphasis on Cyber Security uplift and empowerment.

Susana holds a Bachelor's in Computer and Information Science from the University of South Australia, a Postgraduate in Data Science & Cyber Security from Griffith University, and a Master's in Cyber Security - Leadership & Governance from the University of New South Wales.

Driven by her passion to bridge the gap between technology and life, Susana is dedicated to empowering non-technical communities with vital cyber safety and awareness. As an advocate for inclusion, accessibility, and clear communication, her goal is for everyone to navigate the digital world with confidence and security.